Praise for Al Ortolani:

"...the wild bitterness/in our throats" could be used as a summary for Al Ortolani's beautiful and zestful new collection of poems, *Swimming Shelter*. However, a summary of the book is going to fall far short of this vast and passionate volume. There is so much to capture, sense, hear, feel and visualize in the words, sounds, silence, and devices like metaphors in these poems. In *Swimming Shelter*, you will find the beautifully human crawl into the next poem, the next chaos, a new meditation. Yes, a meditation on life, death, mystery, clay pots and literature. This powerful book is full but it is not the last word. It is literally an invitation from Mr. Ortolani for everyone to keep crawling, keep writing, continue reading. His collection of poems is a lovely example of thriving in the midst of surviving as he tells us on page 158, "Chaucer should have been enough for one/plague." Mr. Ortolani picks up the mantel of Chaucer and shows us abundant thriving in the throws of, yet another, deadly human condition."

-Michael Poage, writer of twelve collections of poetry and Fulbright English Language teaching fellow (virtually) at Walailak University, Thailand, spring, 2021.

More Praise for Al Ortolani:

"Al Ortolani's poems are stuffed with expressive details that place the reader into the poems. This work speaks volumes about the isolation that each person is still feeling; isolation that is not easily integrated into the human psyche. Ortolani describes the "new life" we lead in ways that define his unique style. All poems are universal, and they latch onto the reader as the reader latches onto the hope that is embedded within each poem. A young boy fishes by himself, a couple enjoys a solitary picnic, the author sings to sparrows in the park, ticks are picked off the family dog, a husband covers his wife's flower garden during a late frost – these are all acts of solitary kindness and satisfaction that the world has been forced to adjust to during the age of COVID, and the author majestically describes these tiny miracles in a collection of poems that stretch from March 23, 2020 to June 30, 2020. Like many of us, Ortolani reverts to old memories and replays them through the poems; poems about when the world was the old normal and people were allowed to interact. This book serves as a testament to humans coping during unprecedented times."

- Carmel L. Morse, author of *Bloodroot*

"Al Ortolani's latest book , *Swimming Shelter: 100 Days of Corona Virus*, is a collection of 100 poems written on 100 successive days during the Covid-19 pandemic. The poems, published daily on Facebook, linked by tone, craft and compassion created a vital digital community because they speak to everyone in isolation, without pretense, with compassion, humor and clarity. "

-John Knoll, *Black Mesa Blues* (Spartan Press, 2020)

Swimming Shelter
100 Days of Coronavirus

To Harlotti In wich ti... In thank you

An Exercise in the American Crawl

by Al Ortolani

Kansas City — Spartan Press — Missouri

Spartan Press
Kansas City, Missouri
spartanpress.com

Spartan
Press

Copyright ©Al Ortolani, 2020
First Edition: 1 3 5 7 9 10 8 6 4 2
ISBN: 978-1-952411-39-7
LCCN: 2020952071

Cover art: *Night Swimming* by Jacque Allen Forsher,
www.jacqueforsher.com
Author photo: Sherri Ortolani

Acknowledgments:

A Thanks,

To Spartan Press and Jason Ryberg for believing in this project enough to push it into print in 2020; to the Kansas City Writers Place; to the many on Facebook who followed these poems, at times, workshopping them as they appeared; to Jacque Forsher for her Night Swimming; to my family, children, and grandchildren;

and to my wife Sherri for giving me the space to write.

TABLE OF CONTENTS

March

April

May

June

Author's Note:

The idea for writing one poem a day for 100 days emerged slowly. In March, as we sheltered in place, I discovered that putting poems on Facebook allowed me to communicate with an immediacy that I usually only enjoyed at public readings. It tasted like bacon, like strong coffee. Naively, I thought 30 days would cover the worst of the pandemic.

As I considered shutting down my daily posts, returning to sending poems out to small presses, I experienced a sense of loss, of isolation, that troubled me. I kept writing and posting, finding that I needed the electronic human contact more than a vetted publication with little feedback. Consequently, these poems have been self-published only on my Facebook platform, and on occasion, on the Kansas City Writer's Place website.

In *Swimming Shelter* the poems are arranged chronologically as they appeared. Little has been done to revise, except for an occasional word choice selection or punctuation edit.

I wrote each morning. Usually, stopping only when the poem was finished. A few appeared with an immediacy that surprised me. Other times, I worked off and on throughout the day, giving them up to the internet late at night, but seldom before I was satisfied. This went against the grain of my personal writing process, as I prefer to edit only after days or weeks have passed, letting the poems cool for the critical cold eye. Self-publication scared me, sort of like the time in junior high school, when I accidentally kicked off my penny loafer into the middle of the basketball court during a game. Ninth graders dribbled around my sad shoe like they might a mouse from the biology lab.

The true embarrassment was that I'd forgotten to change my socks after gym class, and so there I was, swinging my dumb foot from the balcony in a sweat-stained sock. Essentially, my social life was ruined, and I became a poet.

I'd like to thank Facebook readers who followed my posts, especially those who commented on what they read. Their words and emojis, likes and loves, let me feel like a village poet, sitting around a smoky fire, probably Irish, weaving words, inventing stories.

I kept the organic character of original diction in place. The use of quarantine instead of stay-at-home or sheltering-in-place is an example of learning terminology, new words for a new time. The inaccuracies are honest. These poems are not all about Covid-19, per se, but all of them, for better or worse, were discovered while swimming in shelter, crawling for calm water.

For the Pittsburg High School Class of 1970,
Wisely Scrubbing Their 50th Reunion
During the Pandemic

Swimming Shelter

There is knowing too little
and too much

in the quiet

as she swims
            out of herself,

a cloud   merging
            with clouds.

March

With or Without Me

Sunlight finally bleeds
through the overcast.
Daffodils brighten the winter mulch,
a forsythia whip, a purple crocus.
Birdsong, early
in the morning gray,
carries a familiar tune.
So, I've written a thousand
poems to spring. Each year
they tumble like marbles
out of a leather bag.
Yes, it is true. I'm the bag,
tightened all winter with
a draw string, rattling
with heft, browned,
scuffed by the years.

March 23, 2020

Everyone Knows a Guy

My guy has toilet paper, one
hundred rolls tucked away
in his garage. Some of us
know electricians, plumbers,
mechanics, sushi chefs.
When the rest of the city
has resorted to smooth stones
and green moss, I'll be
in contact with my guy,
bartering, trading my mother's
China, place setting by place
setting, then the gravy bowl,
the sugar and creamer,
the tea pot. My guy, well,
he's my ace in the hole.

March 24, 2020

Gunslinger

Last night I finally fell asleep
about the time I heard the early
birds chirping in the trees.
My first thought was WTF—
thinking of worms
before the sun. But then it
occurs to me that I'm out of sync,
up all night, sleeping all day.
If I was young, a player,
so to speak, catting around
like a testosterone salesman,
I'd understand, showcase
the swagger, wear cool boots,
a sleeveless t-shirt to display
the suntanned guns. Instead,
I check out the clock, blurred
red without my glasses, pinch
the bridge of my nose.
The city's stay-a-home-order
has turned the streets into
a Stephan King novel. Talk radio
claims the death toll is rising.
I fish my Tony Lamas
from the shadows of the closet.
I step into the middle of 87th Street

at high noon, Woody Allen legs like sticks
of muscle. The beautiful saloon girl
with the Winchester watches
the rooftops. Our imaginary dog
waits to be named in episode two.

March 25, 2020

Distance Between Sparrows

So, my wife and I have been
self-quarantined for the better
part of a week, and I ask her
if she'd like to go out to dinner.
She's been one step away from crazy
so she agrees immediately.
We drive to the little fast food
spot across the interstate,
the one with the middle eastern
manager who plays reggae
through the sound system
while hand delivering burger orders
like an Italian waiter.
We can only use carry-out since
that's the new law, and probably
necessary, considering the pandemic.
So, we take our sack of burgers
and fries outside to a concrete table
that I've never seen used during
normal times. This way we're
not inside the restaurant, but not
really outside either. Before I've
opened the ketchup packets, the manager
eases out of the side door and sits
at the other table which is easily
six feet to our left. He sips a cup
of coffee and begins to sing

an old lullaby from his home country.
We applaud when he's done. Smiling
shyly into his black coffee, he nods
a little and returns the way
he came. My wife wipes a tear
from her eye. We leave a tip
under a rock that I scoop up
from the drive-through. There's
no wind, probably it'll stay put
until he comes out again
to light a cigarette and watch
the parking lot fill with sparrows.

March 26, 2020

St. Francis Kissed Lepers

I return a box of mail order
wet wipes to local shipping.
(No alcohol, my wife explains.)
Two customers at a time
are allowed inside the shop. The third,
an attractive woman
with an oversized envelope
waits at the door. I step up
to a folding table, the kind
I use at garage sales, so there's
two counters, set safely
six feet apart. Usually, there's banter.
That's why I use these guys.
I sign in with a tablet
at the first table. A plastic
"crime scene" tape cordons
the risk zone. I'm thinking
I need to lift the tape over my head
to reach the familiar built-in
counter ahead when I notice
a plastic bin, being pushed
through the air by a harried looking
employee. Place your package
in the crate, sir, he says.
I drop my wet wipes into the bin.
Receipt? He asks.
It's a financial transaction,

so yes, a receipt. Immediately,
the same plastic bin is shoved
through the safe air, my receipt
like an eviction notice, a solitary
essential, a leper's slice of bread.
In leaving, I notice the woman again.
She's now ringing a small bell,
envelope pressed to her face.
St. Francis kissed lepers, but
neither of us breathe.

March 27, 2020

Self-Quarantined with Squirrels' Nests

Throughout the winter
the leaves fall, not crazily
like in autumn, but as with
a scalpel, the blade of ice
and snow that accompanies
the dark months. By spring,
the few remaining leaves
are pushed out by new growth,
pressured by the ensuing generation
to drop, to make space.
With late March, I find
squirrels' nests, positioned high,
tucked in the forks, leaf clumps
riding the naked branches,
wads of yesterday. I drag
my lawn chair out of the garage
and warm myself in the sun.
The wind lifts my gray hair,
rakes the edges of the leaves
that still package the nests.
Somewhere in the distance
a lawn mower trims
a ragged lawn. I pull my hat
tighter against my brow.
There is no reason to move.
Only sitting tempers change.

Children's voices, not mine,
but those who've taken their
places, remind me of the whittling
edge of time. When finally,
I leave this aluminum chair,
it blows sideways, scraping
the concrete driveway
as if with fingernails.

March 28, 2020

First Mowing with Sciatica

My lawn mower chews up
the spring grass, sucks
the green like rich sativa
into a canvas bag. I debated,
whether to collect the clippings,
or let them blow, choosing neatness
over reconstituting the soil.
It is this way in the suburbs, often
manicure wins over nurture.
At the edge of the flower garden,
I pause, surprised by the Teton granite
that I tossed into the mulch last summer,
a stone the size of my fist,
souvenir of mist and pine, gray
with gleaming white striations.
I roll a sandy-colored geode
up next to it, and then position
a chunk of bleached Hawaiian coral
between the two. A Zen garden
which our dog-children will overturn
at the next family supper.
They are fur-balled Shivas, robust
sciatics, anxious to run the lawn.
If they had wings, they'd join
the blue jays, chase the doves
into the evergreens, banter with crows.

How can I be annoyed
except through narrow mindedness?
It is as much their nature
to overturn, as it is mine to arrange,
to plant what grows, even stones
and dried coral. Today is Sunday.
I wind the orange extension cord
like a climbing rope along my forearm,
between my palm and elbow,
a sign of the cross, a genuflexion.
Each day is a day of prayer,
holy in either sun or cloud.

March 29, 2020

Arkansas Vulture

One afternoon on the upper
Buffalo, I sat in the sun, drying
my wet suit, paddle at rest,
the standing waves
hypnotically still, deceptive
in the rushing current. I opened
a can of Vienna sausage,
and instantly, a vulture,
slope-shouldered and monk-cowled,
flapped his wings from his perch
thirty yards downstream.
His flight was so sudden, so precise,
that I sensed he'd heard the wheeze
of my opening can, or smelled
the breath of factory meat
before I did. We shared
the same sunlight, the same
rain-flushed river, yet,
his attentiveness was more
alert than mine, his wingtips
as much a part of the river
as the wave-slapped willows,
the warming limestone.
Once, stoically positioned
like a question mark, he now
circled on an invisible string,
an exclamation, it seemed, in the
silence that follows sound.

March 30, 2020

In My Search for a Poem Today

I became engrossed in the word pandemic,
and how its roots may cross with pandemonium,
or "all demons," as I've understood it to mean
from the Latin, or was it the Greek? However,
pandemic, rather than "all demon," refers to
"all people," with demos, like the word demo-
cratic, etc., thwarting my theme, dammit, on
the demon in disease, the chaos from Milton's
palace. Alas, Billy Collins, I'm self-quarantined.
You, who can find in a dictionary the Muse's
thumbs up—my lanyard weaving is clumsy
with loosened plastic strands, failed keychains.
Today's mnemonic, my Proust cookie, o
Madeline, is but a saltine, an oyster at that.

March 31, 2020

April

Isolated at a City Park

I find a road marked
No Outlet and drive
to the turn around.
A boy fishes in a small
pond. A young couple
spreads their blanket,
and then empties a sack
with a sandwich.
From my distance, it
appears to be a 12 inch
submarine. I have
a pair of binoculars,
but I'm saving them
for red-headed
woodpeckers. Along
the ridge, the local
airplane club becomes
one with their
Piper Cubs, controlled
spins, calculated
dives. Naked,
except for gym
shorts, a man
practices Tai Chi
with a hockey stick.
Up, then down the slope,
he raises one arm,

then the stick, sets
a leg, twists
his torso easily.
There's much
I don't understand
in his muscled gravity,
my jacket zipped
until the sun reaches
my bones. When I close
my eyes, the earth slows,
resonates with one
less sensation.
The woodpecker
I came to watch
beats lazily
on a log drum.
I follow him
until one of us
disappears.

April 1, 2020

Plague Doctor at Sonic with Dandelions

I think about buying
one of those long-beaked
plague masks which
are being advertised
on Facebook. They
stir a collective
memory, a haunting
like basement stairs,
crawl spaces, spiders
under pillows. I'd like
to ride down 87th Street
to Sonic on my Honda,
order two hamburgers
and a Diet Coke. I'd
pay my ticket with cash
without speaking, enjoy
the car hop waiting
for a voice to explain
the cure. Hundreds
of dandelions
spot the uncut lawn,
scented for the beak, cheap
weeds for a girl's
necklace, a boy's bouquet
to a distracted mother.
I once ate dandelion
blossoms, deep-fried

like calamari. The yellow
petals, a thousand
strong, cracked through
the breading. Even
with salt, we gagged
at the perfume,
the wild bitterness
in our throats.

April 2, 2020

Curb Side Groceries

Cold rain has been falling
since late last night. This morning,
icicles hang like pinky fingers
from the deck railing. My wife
has ordered our groceries
online. We park behind
a red sign on the west side
of the parking lot. A clerk searches
for the head of the queue. She walks
car to car with a clipboard.
One woman claims she's been
sitting in her Buick for an hour. In time,
an old guy, shivering in a wind breaker,
pushes a two-wheeler up to the back
of our Rav4. He butchers something
polysyllabic, which could be
an Italian surname. I open the hatch,
and we load half of my wife's order,
the rest unavailable. Wind whips
more rain across the parking lot,
the old guy rocks the two-wheeler
out of pothole. I tip him all the ones
we could dig out of our rat holes.
My wife insists they should go
in a plastic Ziploc. So, he won't
want to open this, I ask?
She ignores me. I don't say

another word. The old guy, who
I've begun to call Andy,
is startled by the gesture.
He smiles through his blue lips. Maybe
he needed a Ziploc after all.

April 3, 2020

While Cutting Classes, I Discover the Spanish
Flu in a Rural Kansas Cemetery

What they didn't know
killed them in 1918, the strain
from Kansas named after the Spanish,
the soldier, the nurse, the farmer,
the shop keeper, white stones
rain-smoothed, sun-bleached
like old newsprint. I understood
motorcycles in 1970, dirt roads
stretching like strands of fence wire
out of Kansas, out of the town
where my parents kept food
on our plates, blankets
on our beds. You can be
whatever you choose,
they insisted, be good, obey God,
go to school. These graves
seemed improbably
peaceful in spring, poems below
cedars, below daffodils, young
in 1918, God
at a man and woman's side,
a bag of camphor
around their necks, the wind
in their lonely prayers.
Tomorrow will be different.
I will know more.
We will know more.

April 4, 2020

Essential Business

There's ice on the mailbox. The ornamental
plum in the rock garden rattles stiffly
as if encased in Saran Wrap. The man
in the trench coat and stocking cap
holds up a small sign, so creased
and wet with rain, that I cannot
make out the words. Stopping the car
around the corner, I walk back to where
he stands, back to me, facing the coming
traffic. Hey buddy, I say, handing him
the smallest bill I have in my wallet.
Anything helps, he answers. The old fear
that I've been fleeced, suckered
by a con, nags at me. Thanks brother,
he says again. My car is still running,
the heat from the vents, blowing warm
against my Patagonia jacket, my
seventy-dollar Gatsby cap.

April 5, 2020

Fred's One Stop Small Engine Repair

No wife, no son, a daughter
named Martha, married to a taxidermist
in Joplin. Born between wars
and raised with a basic education,
I can read, write a letter, do
long division. Lawn mower blades
are my specialty, good rates, free
with the motor tune up. Keeps food
on the table, Chicken Mary's dinner
on Sunday afternoons. I've read
everything Zane Grey has written,
and I'm working my way through
a cardboard box of Louis L'amour.
I don't drink. Smoke Pall Mall. Take
coffee black. I collect duck
statues. Started when I was a boy.
I keep them on the mantle of the fireplace
that hasn't drawn smoke for years.
Someday, Martha will sweep them up
with the dust balls. One of them,
the green headed mallard, is worth
fifty bucks. That's what I heard
from the owner of a Toro 4-stroke.
He said I had something there,
a duck among ducks.

April 6, 2020

Passover

The streets have been as quiet
as clay pots in winter. Even rush hour
is a plugged garden hose, a trickle of wrens,
an escadrille of starlings. Time today
for coffee at the window, buttered toast,
a husband to pour his wife a second cup,
for her to touch his shoulder
in passing. By mid-morning, he leashes
the dog, and they walk the sidewalk to
the park. Helicopters spin from the branches.
Even in pandemic, sparrows splash
their reflections in puddles. Neighbors
embrace without touching. Doorways
are painted with the blood of lambs.

April 7, 2020

Out of the Nest Feeding

I woke up alone this morning,
my wife, having already left
for her three mile walk along
Mill Creek. I stumbled
down to the kitchen to find
it spotless in the late
morning sun. She's left
a cup of coffee in the pot
for Jesus. I take it instead.
The savior is a giving sort,
more prone to herbals anyway.
We slept with the windows open,
the attic fan sucking the
pink moon through the bedroom.
So far, there's been a sense of ease
in the sunlight today, the release
of a single motorcycle changing gears
on 87th Street. Maybe, all is well.
Maybe the two fledgling owls
Mrs. Good found at the base
of a dead tree will survive,
a plastic wood duck house
nailed below the failing nest.
She's in touch with rescue, all life
under the same sky, mayapples
on the forest floor, the moon herself
ladling light onto paved streets.

April 8, 2020

Clusters

Last night my closest
friend woke with
chest pains. Probably,
we devised, from sleeping
wrong, from too much lifting
in the garden, from the 40%
increase in Kansas
COVID fatalities.
Our streets are curve-
flattened, sparrow-
dappled. A fox,
lopes across the neighbor's
lawn, after eating
the dog's Kibbles. Today,
I drive to the Flint Hills
and bring back a dozen
tumble weeds. I loosen them
on12th and Main. They blow
to the river, bounce back
to Westport, then
along the Santa Fe swales
into Overland Park, an
arching circle, a return
to open skies, to creek-fed
cottonwoods, to crates
of Beecher Bibles.
Kansas law makers

revoke Governor Kelly's
Executive Order
to ban large gatherings
on Easter weekend.
The midwestern Jesus
protects, where in New York
or Chicago or New Orleans
he refused. So great
our wheat field faith
that science be damned. Watch us
pass the wine, the spittle from
the Old Rugged Cross, our children
with open mouths
singing.

April 9, 2020

The Flying Cat

Archie sleeps on the windowsill.
Even when he's awake, he appears
to doze. He never exercises, isn't
interested in mice, licks his fur with
a quiet passion. I'd like to put
wings on him and turn him lose
the way a naturalist might loose
a caged raptor. Surely, he'd fly a little.
Probably, surprised to be sky bound
up with the birds that tease him
through the window. I imagine
that he'd circle the house,
not knowing what else to do,
a cottonwood fluff, a small cloud,
a puff of tobacco from a pipe
Then caught in some wind shear,
he'd screech into the old hedgerow,
scaring the crows, panicking
the squirrels. I don't believe
Archie would fly for long, laziness
skips species like the coronavirus.
Finally, he strut home to his window seat,
wings licked to wedges like
ice cream or soft Velveeta. Once asleep
on the usual windowsill,
he might dream of flight, the fields
retreating below him, in his greatness
his old world falling away
like a can of tuna rolling downhill.

April 10, 2020

At Four in the Morning

coyotes are howling, pups yelping
by the creek, probably
where the current cuts under the street,
the long culvert ensconced by scrub trees,
Ozark stones slick with moss, minnows,
mussel shells. Possibly, they've
found a last sack of happy meals,
tossed from the window
of a Ford. Maybe, tacos,
sauce packets, a tortilla
from a bean burrito. Coyotes
survive on the outskirts of the city,
scrounging refuse, the occasional
ground hog or possum roadkill.
They howl, yelp for society, for clan,
for social distance. Over the past
few weeks, skulking behind the fast food,
the grocery, the Italian deli,
has not provided good hunting.
They've returned to the creek, the small
nail of wildness, extending
like a finger from the Kansas River.
If mankind is ever at a total loss,
coyotes will follow the water, back
to the farmlands, back even further
to the midnight hunt, the dens,
the warrens, the bones from larger kills.

Over two thousand people are predicted
to die tomorrow in the United States.
Researchers claim this, the peak,
from which recovery will begin
in inches. If so, the coyote
will remain secreted with mice and frogs,
emerging when the dumpsters are full,
the alleys flowing. Coyote's wilderness
has no mapped demarcation. There is
no beginning to what has no end,
and no end to fortune.

April 11, 2020

Hewn from a Dogwood

Trouble in sleep last night, so
I wake early on Easter morning.
Heavy rain threatens.
Thunder rumbles. The city is as
still as a whisper, an empty hand,
creased, palm open, cupped
for rain. The dogwood
brightens the window, small
twisted limbs heavy with flower,
neon against the charcoal sky. Four
white petals, a cross blossom,
joined by stamens, anthers and
filaments, pollen grains.
Dogwood legend calls this center
a crown of thorns. On the curve
of each petal is a nail hole,
a stain of red bleeding across the skin.
On the hillsides, the dogwood
punctuates the forest with hope
of early spring, the redbud,
the wild pear, daffodils
resurrected from flood.
Now, the rain, as promised,
begins. I drop an extra
cube of sugar into
my coffee, treat the cat
to a raw egg, beaten
to yellow in his bowl.

April 12, 2020

Eagle Scout as an Old Man

I went out into the garden at dusk
to tie down the sheets that covered
the azaleas. The wind blew ape-shit,
cutting through my jacket and numbing
my fingers. I tied knots
while cussing the twine. Sherri
yelled from the backdoor
to come in, and I thought, no eff-ing way
am I going to let you lose these
bright flowers during a late damn
freeze. I blew in my hands.
The sheets ballooned and whipped
like kites, man-clouds in spitting rain.
Using scraps of hardwood flooring,
garden rocks, fence posts, I tied
the wet sheets at the corners,
and lashed them to the earth. Survival
tents, lean-tos. I was an Eagle Scout
by god. The neighbor's television
filled his window with a Brooklyn
hospital, a line of ambulances, a reporter
in blue plastic. I thought of potato soup.
Sherri opened the door again, flipped on
the porch light, my lower back
seizing up, cramping like it did
when I shoveled topsoil. I hammered
the wooden stake at the base

of the orange azalea one last time,
tossed the quilt
over the pink, hoping
that sodden, it could provide
enough gravity to avoid lifting away
like some airborne manta ray.
Somewhere in the darkness, I'd lost
my pocketknife. The twine ball
had rolled off into the rock garden,
a lump among lumps. It was enough
to pick up my Boy Scout hatchet,
and return to the kitchen's glow,
stooped in mild back pain, fingers
twine-raw, all said, less
pissed off at God than before.

April 13, 2020

Before Vietnam

Once while walking under
the college football stadium, Dana
and I heard gunshots coming
from the ROTC rifle range. We slipped
around back, through a door
that's now a men's john.
We watched two cadets, lying prone,
about where the seats sloped enough
to make you stoop. They were
shooting into a sandpit. Another guy
held a cigarette over a clipboard.
Unconcerned about our presence,
they asked if we'd ever shot an M-1.
I hadn't. Dana didn't answer. In turn
we lay on a blanket, rifle resting
on a sandbag. The steel barrel
angled towards a paper target.
The soldier with the clipboard folded
his arms around me, helping steady
the weight, level my aim. He guided
my finger to the trigger.
We pulled together, the recoil
jolted my shoulder, something stung
my eye, but the thud
of the bullet hitting
troubled me the most.

Just a whump and spray
of sand, it felt as consequential
as a rumor, as a small lie that I couldn't
comprehend. We laughed
all the way home, promising
not to tell our mothers,
but I told my dad anyway. He said,
they probably knew what they were doing.
The M-1 was the best rifle made.

April 14, 2020

Sherri's Birthday in a Time of Pandemic

On your birthday, the jewelry
store, the florist, even Taco Bell
is closed due to pandemic.
I should have considered Amazon
or a socially distanced singing telegram,
but I was surfing Netflix,
and scrounging toilet paper.
So, I bought you this tank top

at Walmart for $9.99. In truth,
it isn't special,
until you slip it on.

April 15, 2020

Spinning Honey

When there are too many words
for clear thought, like, for instance, bees
swarming a cottonwood,
sentences, paragraphs, yes, the message
gets lost. With a blank brain,
there are no words at all, a flat stone
in a creek bed, both dusty and dusted off.
Maybe here, in emptiness
is the place to begin. Creek beds
fill with rain, with runoff,
whereas in a bee tree, the storm
of flight is disconcerting, a swatting
of small dramas, bee upon bee
connecting the whole, the single-sexed
workers, clambering the bee ball,
the queen at the heart, protected,
sequestered like the one clear thought
on an otherwise busy day.
The tree limb bends with the gravity
of bee weight. Here's the cottonwood
at the creek's edge, and then again
below the ridge of the city, the hum of bees,
the hum of traffic, light in pandemic,
the glass and steel, the carbon print
of a generation, all of this
part of the greater city, the topography
of Kansas, Missouri, the Midwest,

the continent, good and diverse,
all bee glade, voice drummed,
at rest and in flight simultaneous.
The earth herself throbs with
consciousness, with all life, sentient
and vegetable. Even this
stone below the bee tree, smoothed,
rain-washed, swarms with molecules,
atoms, and electrons, the same
as flesh, as bone, as breath itself.
So, where is clarity, the beeline,
the queen's flight, the hot knife?
Each morning flexes new muscle,
the spinning comb, the centrifuge,
the wrist and ankle of industry,
bending in dance.

April 16, 2020

Scraping Mud Daubers

Standing on the iron
bench, I slide the
putty knife blade
under the insect mud,
and pop the organ pipes,
one by one, onto the
porch. It takes a few
hard scrapes to clear
what remains, to smooth
the ridge from a season's
industry. Dust sprinkles
my jacket, grays
my hair even more.
I breathe the old mud,
sucking last summer's
garden into my lungs. It is
not offensive, mild
as tilled dirt, a
neighborhood smell,
the row of familiar
homes, once ticky taks,
now exuding years
of add-ons, revisions
of blueprints, garden
walls, kitchens
opened to great rooms.

The boy who grew up
in the charcoal multi-level
graduated, packed off
to college last August.
His parents, Tom
and Marsha, trucked
their empty nest
to a townhouse near
the golf course. We spoke
maybe a dozen times
in ten years, waved
frequently at the mailbox,
laughed once at the grocery.
His basketball goal
remains above the garage,
nylon net hanging
by a few strings, the echo
of the ball, dribbled up
the drive, sported
away in wind.

April 17, 2020

One Fat Grackle

Three small fishing boats
motor up the cove this morning,
creasing the lake into the shallows.
Here, the water is warmer, pregnant
with crappie, windfall nests, bundled
winter limbs. One flat bottom works
the lake's edge, trolling the bank, two
fishermen standing, casting, letting
their lines trail. From my vantage
across the cove, they are prehistoric
cranes, afoot in the dawn. All is old.
Tibetan prayer flags without wind,
draped one end to an oak, the other
spiked into the rocks with rebar,
the colors are faded, onion thin
threads frayed to transparency.
A thousand prayers in the Ozarks,
up the cove, the creek, Baptist-fed,
Pentecostal-grown, still, all graves
are catholic at best. In bird flight,
the red tail hawk, the kingfisher,
a sullen dove in the greening
dogwood, a surprise of redbuds
with Hitchcock's starlings, one
fat grackle. A squirrel hurries
up the deck rail. He pauses on
the top post beside the cabin, sees

me standing through his reflection
in the glass door. He leaps
to the nearest oak, negotiates
the prayer flags. In seconds
he's up, bounding
through the branches
until I've lost him.

April 18, 2020

A Knot in the Rope at the Front of My Brain

When I smile,
it tightens as if
bound by kudzu

or briar. There
is nothing pretty
in a squeezed

frontal lobe.
It purples like
cabbage, dries

in the market
near the wrinkled
peppers, the limp

celery. I once read
about a turbaned fakir
who climbed a rope,

hand over hand to heaven.

My hands are cracked
walnuts. They need lanolin,
the softening spittle

of lamb's wool.

April 19, 2020

Tired of Birds

Well, not really birds, but I'm
tired of writing about birds.
Primarily, that's all I've got
most mornings at my window.
Cardinals greet me with song,
which is fine, beats the beeping
watch, but I seldom see them
because I don't want to get
out of bed, or to drag myself
out of sleep too quickly, if at all.
My system, slow as it is, might
get shocked into some sort of
arrythmia or stroke seizure.
So, I listen, and eventually, write.
But like I said, or implied,
I need a new subject, isolated
as I am, as we all are, with
orders to cease and desist in
human interaction. So, it's tough.
No bars. No dancing. No sing-alongs
at karaoke clubs. Yesterday,
I shook hands with an old guy
named Bill. We were discussing
where best to burn leaves
in a crowded neighborhood.
I should probably report him to the cops,
or the WHO, or, at least, Dr. Fauci.

But I took his hand without
a wet wipe, warm and fleshy
like a pork chop. We shook on it,
whatever this "it" is, that men
shake on in brief encounters,
maybe something like, yea,
I know you're alive, and I'm
alive, so let's clasp hands,
acknowledge the inevitable
which could be death. But often,
it's our pork chop lives we recognize,
and the birds that wake us.

April 20, 2020

Rice and Lentils

Little in-depth news coverage
has followed. But according to
CNN, the BBC, Fox, etc.,
six tourists from five countries,
were expelled from their hotel
in the heartland of Beatle yogaville.
They were holed up in a small
mountain cave. Dipping water from,
the Ganges, they were able
to stay clean, hydrated, and holy
on very few rupees per day.
Ready cash had been part of
their problem since the beginning.
Running low on funds, and high
on pandemic restraints, they
couldn't leave and couldn't stay.
I understand caves in India
have been lived in for years. They're
rather posh by cave living
standards, semi dry floors, free
of creeks and blind salamanders,
probably swept clean of bats
on a regular basis. Demand
for caves in spiritual circles
can be high. Young yogis
take what's available, pandemic
or not. It's an ancient thing,

living Gandhi-style, either by choice,
or by circumstance, parsing out
rice and lentils, tsampa and tea.
I've slept in a cave before.
Really, it wasn't bad, except for
the diving bats, and the lovers
in the sleeping bag
the stalactite over, who kept
rediscovering themselves.

April 21, 2020

Sneeze

I woke today with a blank page
and a nearly blank mind. To get
much blanker would probably
entail a religious experience, a death,
so to speak, which is also
a religious experience, well, dying is,
since death, if you're like
many atheist-inclined moderns,
is a blankness without experience,
concept free, a preposition, an of…
without an object. It's difficult
to imagine, since all imaginings
use things, even cats like Schrodinger's,
curled in a box, alive and dead
simultaneously. Sometimes, I prefer
to use the word oblivion, when
I attempt to explore the lack
of consciousness which
some say is death, like being
blown to smithereens, inexplicitly,
by let's say, a gas truck, a rush of
incinerating flame, a swoosh.
Usually, oblivion ushers less drama,
like with anesthesia, a few deep breaths of
ether before a tonsillectomy, a drip of
whatever doctors use today, say
from an IV in hernia repair.

There's nothing afterwards.
A deep hush. A falling. A death.
The same is true in love, the
little death of lovers, la petite mort,
heart-stopping, sweaty, soul-clenching.
But more commonly, there's the sneeze,
the cosmological ka choo.
Oblivion curves with the cherry
blossom branch, as much in sunlight
as shadow, or, yes, like a butterfly
mistaken for a leaf, suddenly
lifting with orange wings. Ask any
student of Zen, the moment of oblivion
is union, the one hand clapping,
a twig moving on spindly legs.

April 22, 2020

Rodeo Clown

Walking home after work, stinking
of French fries and toilet cleanser,
I'm mindful of my midnight curfew,
the jazzed-up hot rods in the

parking lot of Griff's Burger Bar.
Tony sits on a fender of his pickup,
his Schlitz out of the brown bag.
The only senior in speech class

smiles when I pass, nods with
his chin. For a moment, I'm hanging
in western boots, mop-haired,
Marlboro trapped between

my fingers, the next few years
of confused decisions behind me.
I'm too tough to be messed with,
even my parents have quit

telling me what to do. My girlfriend
is like a deer, her reputation wild,
as desirable as the word yes.
She slides across the seat, next

to my arm when I drive. I'm casual
with the steering wheel. Going nowhere
together, we wave indifferently
when I pass myself on Broadway.

April 23, 2020

Finding the Trillium

while walking a wooded trail
is rare, and frustratingly unfulfilling,
if that is your day's goal. A friend said,
it is better to walk with soft eyes,
scanning the forest floor
without intention, as much enthralled
by lichen and moss
as the three petaled trillium,
to stumble on beauty
when led by an owl's feather
or by the drumming woodpecker.
The narrowed eye is best used
when lacing heavy boots, rather, than
in leaving yourself unshod.

April 24, 2020

Water Snake

My grandsons wade a creek
that feeds the Kansas River.
The older, in some intrepid zone,
moves off downstream, negotiating
the rocks below the surface,
the sudden drop-offs, the play
of wind-dappled waves. The younger
boy trails behind, at first trying
to keep up, then slowing to a pace
that keeps him from falling.
Already, he has bloodied his shin,
been swallowed up to his navel.
There's an importance in exploration
that I don't care to reel in,
so, I follow at a safe distance,
the low water bridge now
well behind. Frequently,
the older boy turns
to see if I am following. I can't
tell if I'm an annoyance
or a comfort. He spots a water snake,
slipping through the current.
He points. The younger scans
the reflection along the bank,
troubled, rock clambering, unable
to locate the snake. His cousin
keeps walking. Both are too young

to turn loose. Maybe I'll tell them
the story of Lewis and Clark,
months discovering what lays
behind the next bend.

April 25, 2020

American Standard

Have you ever noticed how a house
has a life of its own? This one that
my wife and I share creaks

and groans with middle age, only
a half century, but old by many
housing standards. Today, it is

the plumbing, the mix of plastic,
copper, and cast-iron drains,
thumping, knocking in the walls

as the week's laundry agitates, rinses.
Windows vibrate in storm. A few,
hard to open, fall on their own accord.

The humming light in the bedroom
should belong to Satchel Paige. Once
the switch is turned, I slip into bed

before electricity leaves the bulb.
Late at night, the toilet chants,
an American Standard with

bubbly vowels. In the two-by-fours
wood screws complain of age,
humidity, summer heat. They back

out of contracts, their petitions
muted by sheetrock and insulation.
Occasionally, I hear something fall.

I open closets, check the doors,
take a flashlight to the basement
where the boxes sleep.

April 26, 2020

Aftermath

My mother heard someone
walking on the floor above her.
It was the middle of the night,

and as a light sleeper, she always
listened for her children, waking
when they should be sleeping.

This was many years ago, before
brain bleeds, TIAs, and dementia
wagged her like a puppet, and

many years ago, she was fearless,
we assumed. She took the stairs
to the living room, to face down,

not one of her children, sneaking in
late, or sneaking out early, but
an interloper, blue-jeaned, t-shirted,

standing over her collection of glass
elephants, the little light in the room
caught in their trunks, the flap ears,

the needle point tusks. She stiffened
her spine, house coat trailing:
What was he thinking? I could have

had a gun. By this time, my father
had pulled himself out of bed,
groggy, unable to find his baseball

bat or his catcher's mitt.
Together, they watched the thief,
if that's what he was, leaving

as he'd come, quietly, in the middle
of the night, lit like a scalpel
for months to come.

April 27, 2020

The New Normal

When all this is over,
we meet at the park
and toss a Frisbee around.
I run towards the lake,
and you lead
with a slicing spin
near the duck house.
Friends from Facebook
arrive from beyond

the digital trees. Some walk,
others have carpooled.
How much taller we look
in person! Multi-colored disks
unravel the sky. Some,
borne like planets, spin

a solar system of hope.
Laughter replaces lol, and lmao
litters the park with detached butts,
clapping like seals at the irony
of the joke. A spring day
exists in real time, lilacs,

paintbrush, violets,
as vivid as the
photographs
we so desperately
like.

April 28, 2020

Last Wish

At death, I review
the security footage
of my life, complete
with sound, replay,
and editing
capabilities, and as
a package deal, there's
buttered popcorn.
I'm going to make an

afterlife of this
remake, cutting
and splicing
for the redemption of it.
Take, for instance,
Big Larry in fourth grade,
who used to knock
me around. I'd
like to give him

duck feet, and small
ineffective wings.
He would quack. Teachers
would have me line up
first for recess. I'd kick
Nancy's ass at Tetherball.

Childhood would be
a comedy, the rest of it,
well, the process of script
writing, takes and
retakes, could go on

for another lifetime,
and maybe it does,
which is fine,
since I really have
no place else
to go. Frankly,
I fear the footage

is looped, erased
every 24 hrs.
like above a pawn
shop counter, or back
by the fast food
at the Quick Trip,
and there I'd be caught
with the mustard,
my mouth stuffed
with a hotdog
for eternity.

April 29, 2020

Forever Together

My wife is the gardener, but
she wants me to help her dig a hole
for a new bush she picked up

at the nursery. I'll shovel away
the dirt and sandstone
while she separates the cable

television wire from the roots.
I'll need the axe. She worked
yesterday with a hand spade

and a Boy Scout hatchet. Poor girl.
This is what husbands are for,
especially those who spend the day

with a book on Zen Buddhism,
and then, at night with a Netflix
docuseries on tigers. It's a simple

trade. His back for a shrub.

His under-worked hamstrings
for yellow blossoms, a tit for tat
dead drop for family wiffle balls.

April 30, 2020

May

Plain Talk

I woke at 4:30 this morning and sat
in my over-sized leather chair to write.

>> a chunk of coral for
>>> a thousand years, and now,
>>>> a paperweight

It's a good chair, one that I salvaged
from a neighbor's dumpster. Probably,
it is too comfortable. I noticed this
right away this morning. No sooner
had the cushion compressed, then I began
to settle into the hypnogogic loop. That is
the problem sometimes.

>> there is a word
>>> for this, not yet
>>>> discovered

We try too hard to sequester our "best laid"
from the hurry of the world. We squeeze
until the sand drains between our fingers.
I nodded off twice before returning to bed,
my monkey brain clinging to the banana.
One thought stuck, as I kicked
to the surface for the second time,
anxiety is the moon of the city.

>> he died tonight, and I
>>> never heard his name, just
>>>> wind in the branches

I am fortunate with my retirement
intact for the time. I've seen no difference
in the hamburgers I eat. Yes,
condiments of hand sanitizer, face
masks, elbow hugs. As an introvert, by choice,
I do not miss social gatherings. I wish

        coasting tonight
               down the sleeping street,
                      between breaths, my
               mother

to hug my grandchildren, to cook
a large family meal, watch the boys
bat the Wiffle ball, Ava dance
a new routine for her aunts. I have
enough money today, not to be uprooted

        into the old night
               the owl, wings spread,
               swooping
                      where words cannot
                 follow

like an azalea, one that keeps
blooming in the truck bed.

May 1, 2020

Jesus Ate Tilapia

I could write a book about fishing,
even though I've seldom caught
a fish in my life. I have this romantic

notion of sitting on a log at the far
end of a strip pit, pole extended,
nylon line dropped like a question

into my reflection. Sometimes
I'm in a john boat, trolling
the shaded waters, again the pole

extended, this time like a hand
calming the waters. But that's
about where the fishing

stops, since like I said, I've never
been lucky with fish. Mostly,
they steal my bait, or tease me with

their cloud shadows. I admire
their poetry, their understanding
of the depths. On the few occasions

when a bass has set the hook,
I've been dismayed, torn
from the peace of it by the curved

jaw, the suffocating eye, the panting gills.
True, I catch and release. Even that
sportsman's kindness gives me pause

as I wheedle the barb from a cellophane
lip, better maybe to eat what is caught
like the honest carnivore, a ballpeen

to the head. There is a slippery slope
to fish empathy, barely sentient as they are.
Once sliding to the water's edge,

there are deer, Diana's doe, Bambi's
mother. Eventually, even cows, the
face of the Hindu Om. And what

about chickens, and yes, turkeys
as dumb as watering cans. In time,
I'm suffering remorse

for every sandwich at the deli,
the ham & cheese on rye, slammed by
the bolt, slit by the knife.

May 2, 2020

Owl in the Sycamore

The night window opened, the air
cool, but without edge, a soft
Kansas humidity to it, one that
creases when the owl calls.
I wait for a reply, his mate possibly,
but his soliloquy remains unanswered,
as singular as a wing feather. The dog
guards the firepit, legs folded
like the Sphinx, head alert. She rests
in the old pose, at once immediate
and ancient. The yard piques her
interest with rabbits and squirrels.
She eats dry food, bloodless
from a stainless bowl. Wildness
is only on hold in the city, kept
at bey by wooden fences
and porch lights. Our children
are safe in their beds. We paint the
bedroom walls with rollers, talismans
from Sherwin Williams. The best
books explain night terrors,
adjudicate sharpened stakes, color
each species of owl.

May 3, 2020

The Isolation of Peonies

If I sit in this room for much longer,
I'll have written all there is to write
about the window to my left, the one
with the dogwood, once in flower, but now,

greened over, leafed out. Another
rain bulldogs in from the west.
It's been building, a roiling sediment,
since the first thunder an hour ago.

The trees sway, the fulling leaves
upside down, exposing their legs
like girls in windblown dresses. The cat
meowing at the door, the ear-popping

dip in pressure. An enclave of peonies,
heavy-headed, bows like penitents.
Again, I am a face at the window, the old
storm blowing from the unknown

into that which is hidden. Hail clatters
against the glass-topped table.
My daughters photograph the piled ice,
and message it to family.

May 4, 2020

Correct Grammar

It was taught, never use a pronoun
until first you've established the noun.
That's what I learned in English 101.
The "it" rule, when applied to each

paragraph, gave cohesion to meaning.
A few courses later, probably
the American Short Story, I learned
the Latin, in medias res, which as

a device to the best coming of age
narratives hatched the thick of it.
When Barefoot Mick showed in class
on eggshells, straight from the

middle of things,

antecedents grew redundant. Mick
refused shoes until winter, preferred
denim shirts and wide-bell jeans.
He wore a brass bracelet, fingered

on his wrist, a Montagnard for the nerves.
His "It" was the arch to every declining narrative,
poems without clarifying nouns, mumbled
slang, an LZ, in country, a click.

His was hell to edit. The "It" we didn't see,
kept distant, smoky with burnt orange.
We could only imagine
it as he lived it.

May 5, 2020

Lifting the Stay-at-Home

Air hammers pop the rooftops like a troupe
of river dancers on plywood. Now, a cement truck,
grinds its big drum, filling forms for a new pylon.
The sun brightens, hidden behind gray overcast.
The dog in the doorway lifts his head, only
for a moment, curious. Concrete rattles, slides
the main chute, scraping and tumbling.
The drum turns, spins yards of ready-mix.
The shout of a foreman rises hawk-like
into the neighborhood trees, the voice of work
tuned to trunnion roll. He levers the earth today
with fingers crossed, hand on his hip, hard hat
cocked, the diesel of a paycheck,
beer at the end of the day, good health
and muscled shoulders, vibrant in the irises,
the most feminine of flowers.

May 6, 2020

Fetching Sticks

The lawn is heavy with clippings.
Even though I ran the bagger
as my wife prefers, the grass
is too thick, deepened by rain
and late sun. The new dog, a pup,
rescued from a Missouri
roadside, pauses from chasing
the mower around the yard
to scratch another tick from behind
his ear, or maybe from the soft spot
where his neck joins his jaw.
I can't tell. We've been picking them off
since we brought him home. This new
one is fat, leaves a streak of blood
down his white jaw. I dug another
yesterday the size of a grape,
smearing my fingers with dog blood
as it burst. The dog, yet
unnamed, takes to my wife.
He follows her around the house,
cocks his head when she speaks
from the next room. This morning,
after the lawn is cut, the two of them
are going to practice with the leash
which he only fights when she
wishes to turn right or left,
or for that matter, move any direction

that he hasn't decided first.
She speaks to him like she might
a four-year old child. He listens
like he gets it, and I suppose he does
get what's important, the bowl
of dried food, the clean blanket, the
reassuring syllables from her lips.
This wasn't his world yesterday,
except for the ticks and the fleas.
One ear, notched with a V, is healed.
Other scars are deeper, braced
with roadside, thorns and buckshot.
He knows what I suspect
of abandonment, forgets it
more quickly then
I can imagine.

May 7, 2020

Three Thoughts for Thursday

Convinced that today is Thursday,
I make my plans while still in bed.
My wife, heavy-footed in the kitchen,
is impatient for me to get up.
When I check my phone to see
if the world has imploded overnight,
I notice that Thursday is actually
Friday, and somehow, I have missed
twenty-four hours. My first thought
is that Verizon has been hacked
by North Koreans, the second, that
I have slept an entire revolution
of the globe. The third thought
is to make do with Friday, since it's
one day closer to Saturday, which
likely, is just as the day before.

May 8, 2020

Below Highway 76

For two days,
I returned to the rocks below
the bridge, each time choosing
to portage, boat on my shoulder,
paddle in hand, now, a mosquito bat,
a perch for damselflies. Weariness
must have forced me on, the joke
in the comedy of myself, as much
as the paddlers who'd gone
ahead, now bobbing safely in the
eddy, talking easily, paddles
relaxed like cigarettes.
When my boat
flipped above the sluice, I wasn't
surprised. A dozen eyes
were on me, my kayak swept
like a stick, a campfire faggot,
half-burned, toppling in flood.
Somewhere was rescue, a throw rope
unraveling from a bag. If ever
there was forever, it was now,
alone with myself, at last,
where the poem begins.

May 9, 2020

Mother's Day

Our rescue dog chewed-up my best
poetry last night, Ted Kooser, Billy
Collins, Seamus Heaney. He even dog-eared
my WS Merwin, yes, the old Buddhist
himself. The dog is a pup, forgivable.
I had let the two of us fall asleep
in my upstairs man cave. He prefers a pillow
for his head, and the books were stacked
on the floor. I took the little bed
below the Tibetan Thangka,
and that was that.
When I was a boy, my mother said
that nothing is ever as good, or as bad
as you expect. There's a sense to this
which I've held close to my chest.
The dog has a terror of the kennel.
I can't bear to lock him at night,
and, so, I've got to stand watch
and pay for my weak discipline. My mother
died four years ago. Hers was
a painful turn with dementia-charged
hallucinations. I thought about
what she told me as a boy, expecting
better for her, brittle, shrinking
like a late summer iris. She spoke
in whispers. So, I had to bend to her,
catch meaning as it was implied.

But, more to that,
the mother within is the mother of us.
Words are taught secondary to love.
Tone, as the feather
behind the syllable, opens the book,
turns the page, chewed in innocence,
mumbled through pain.

May 10, 2020

Pneumonia

Her father was gone before
she could pronounce
the illness that took him.

One memory
of a sock game, he
juggles them over her head,
just out of reach, snapping
them out of the air, out
of nothing, presto
presto, he slips
them on her feet,
the laughter, piggy toes,
her warm

ankles, one game,
then walking through
a construction site, St.
Luke's, she guesses
in hindsight, the
new cement dusty, still
curing under their feet,
sunlight like linoleum,
scattered lumber,

rooms without doors,
windows with bird flight,
all of it an echo, the
thresholds of change

May 11, 2020

A New Raccoon

I have not washed my hands
so much since, well, since forever,
Soft Soap in the dispenser
by the sink in the kitchen, in the
hall bathroom, in the bedroom
next to the toothbrushes.
On occasion, I don't know what
I'm scrubbing off, cannot say
that I've encountered any
virus-positives on the street,
at the grocery, in driving the car
to the bank teller's window.
It's odd this scrub-down, this
scraping of skin, as if I am a penitent
preparing for communion, a wafer
in the hand, on the tongue, the sip
of wine with the floating host.
I'm not even a good Catholic, a
cafeteria Christian, picking lettuce
from behind the sneeze guard.
My hands are clean, but they do not
sparkle pink. Too many years
have aged them, dry skin, liver spots,
a wart, a scar. Much of the past
cannot be cleaned with soap, the dirt
lies below the skin, like karma,
like a dozen bad decisions, giving in

to yes, instead of no. Allowing no,
when indeed, it was yes. And to think
that my life might depend on Lysol
and warm water, as if all this cleaning
is something novel, a new raccoon
scrubbing mussels in the creek bed.
Like, we haven't known clean skin, since
the first confession, since we knelt
in the box, and the window opened
to the voices of women
on the banks of a river, singing
the old songs, slapping
laundry on rocks.

May 12, 2020

Shooting at Rabbits

Early dawn, the cockcrow is light
through flint glass, a mercury
silvered mirror. All that is
illuminated tilts forty degrees
to the left of sun, behind rooftops,
behind the curve of the horizon.
The smallest birds are flickers
in the highest branches, maples
and oaks, a poplar. The fence
between our yards, weather-worn,
lists with repair. I am the only
one so early, not a light
in a window, the pastel paste
of suburbia deepening with the
approach of rain. We are practiced
at sheltering in place, ankle deep
in the retreat from traffic,
from shopping carts, from the
hand sanitizer displays, already
picked to bone, already gone
the way of an uncle, mother's
Bill, the one with the pencil thin
mustache, who once on a country road,
pulled a .22 single shot from the floorboards,
swung it up in front of my face, and fired
down the crossroad, dust skipping
where he aimed, a rabbit

darting into a stand of tall grass
without a scratch, none
the worse, none the better.
Today, I wait for time to pass.
Morning, rabbit-eared, hesitates
to meet the day, a train in the distance,
and the neighbor, if watching,
parts the curtain
with the barrel of her nose.

May 13, 2020

Averting Catastrophe

Having a dog in the house keeps me waking early.
Before the cat and before my wife. We wander out to
relieve ourselves, he in the bushes or the middle of
the lawn, and I, afterwards behind the lilacs. Then it's
time for breakfast, a couple of scoops of dry dog food
in a stainless-steel bowl. He buries his chin up to this
nose, rattling his dog tag around the rim until the
bowl is empty. In seconds, clean.

a man's face curves
inside the spoon, concave
before coffee

Then, it's back outside, where he trots around the
lawn with his nose in the grass or in the mulch,
occasionally, sniffing the flowers, the shrubs, until if
we're lucky, he squats in familiar fashion and unloads.
This pleases both of us, he bounds towards me as if
full of helium, ready to play, and to drag his chew toys
from the floor of the kitchen to the patio. I can return
to my bedroom, maybe to the desk, maybe to bed,
once coffee is made, once the danger of a landmine is
averted.

ants on the kitchen counter,
bumping shoulders
without apology

The cat shows himself as I open the front door, a night
of insolent catting around. The dog positions himself
just inside the entry, shouldering the second-grade

threshold like a third grader. I push him back a few
inches with my foot and the cat enters. The dog makes
a feint towards him, and the cat swipes at his nose, the
dog retreats a step, but only a step, lunges again more
aggressively. The cat wind mills his claws and the dog
backs up, his butt to the closet, done with the cat. The cat
doesn't wait for a victory lap, but dashes through his small
door into the basement. I check the dog's nose for blood.

newspaper rolled
in blue plastic, rainwater
bleeding into headlines

May 14, 2020

Boomer Remover

The weatherman said that the winds
would pick up today, and blow the rain clouds
eastward through Missouri and into Illinois.

The sun would shine, he promised, for most
of the day. Although cooling, Friday would
be a fine day for flying kites, or unzipping

the covers from the furniture cushions.
But none of that has happened, the rain hangs
around all night, and is still brooding

this morning, the dark sky, thick, sweet even,
like pancake syrup. I am a little bored of writing
poems about weather. It is too predictable

with the Doppler radar, the heavy storms
colored in gold and red. Probably, it is not
weather that tires me, but retirement

as another promise. When the boy
at the grocery sacks my canned beets

next to the canned asparagus shoots, I
explain to him that I used to have his job,
stocking cereal, sacking cream corn, checking

bananas through the analog register. I counted
change, chanted the math, the numbers
adding up like a contract, like a handshake

over a fence. When the good old days (which
were not all that good), get bound up
in the check-out lane, some old men run on

without a period, with just a vague thesis,
comma following comma, until the groceries,
shrouded in plastic, get carried away.

May 15, 2020

The Weekend Mystic

Meditation has taught me to sleep better.
My wife wakes up in the middle of the night,
or maybe, just before the sun rises over

George's house, and she is pretty much done
with the pillow, popping and reshaping it
to fit the contours of her second sleep.

On the other hand, I studied with both
Buddhist and Christian monks, and I don't mean
registering for an online seminar. No,

I traveled some, and sat at the holy feet
of holy men, white sarongs, maroon robes, black
and white vestments. They called their

practices many names, Vipassana, Samatha,
Centering Prayer. I waxed on and waxed off
with Tai Chi, cried in Hatha Yoga.

I once telephoned a Lakota medicine man
to sign up for a Sun Dance piercing. He laughed
and hung up. I learned to breathe,

visualize, and rise with a bell. And I swear
to God, that I now sleep anywhere. Waking
in the night or in the wee hours, I drift

away in my best corpse pose
like a low cloud over a small valley.

May 16, 2020

Ending the High Speed

So, what now, after the chase ends,
your car in a stranger's yard,
a quiet house on a quiet street

where the shade
from the oaks deepens
the hush? Did you unravel the

decisions that led you here, hiding
in the darkest silence,
abandoned, tires shredded

by stop sticks, a gun in the front seat,
a child, crying in the back?
Run to me, the shadows say, find

where the do-over begins.
Run before the rifle speaks,
before the news clip, the story.

Overhead helicopters circle,
searchlights, flattened like lozenges
in the old gardens, climbing

the stone facades, the fences, the
concrete statues, now, as naked
as price tags. This was not

the plan tonight, a dozen police
with handguns, others with
assault rifles, crouched between

hydrangeas, hand signaling
your name through the lilacs.

May 17, 2020

A Good Haiku Is Larger Than a Dog

Today would be a good day for haiku,
even the dog thinks so, after he's had
my wife's best running shoe
leveraged out of his mouth. Cool mornings

are best for haiku, the breeze
and the rain, as linked and indivisible
as seventeen syllables are to paper.
We explain the world to our kids

with names, and later, by identifying
relationships, bird leaving his song
in the wind, etc. It helps to know
that a bird is not a dog, or that a dog

is not the same as a chewed shoe.
Still, it is confusing when kids attend
college to become a poet, or a physicist,
or a shoe salesman, especially, one

who specializes in the shoes that
dogs love. Connection is difficult
to teach, often without a name, and
larger, even than a Google Search.

May 18, 2020

Mulligan

There's nothing in my head today.
I even have trouble focusing on my favorite
Billy Collins' poems. My fingers can't
find the keys on the keyboard
.

For no apparent reason
my computer asks if I wish to save
the page I'm working on. And then
the page disappears, and I'm concerned
for some reason I can't figure, since
this blankness held nothing but intent.
I hope the rest of the day will get better.
I had no plans. It was clear sailing

from morning to midnight.
Maybe I'll crawl back into bed
and start over, calling mulligan
to the knot in the center
of my back, to the ache of waking
with an empty suitcase for a brain, for
the coffee I dribbled down my shirt.
So, I change t-shirts, pour another cup

of coffee. I find my Speedo, the joke
from a landmark birthday. I've never
been to a tanning salon, never had a mulligan
coconut-oiled and glistening with future.

When I return home, my wife will put down
her crossword, and wonder where I've
been all her life. It'll be a moment of
electricity between us. Later, I'll pick up

a guitar and walk to the city park.
No longer needing the Speedo, I'll sing
in key to the sparrows. What a mulligan,
they'll tweet to one another.

May 19, 2020

Walking Stick

Something is ahead of me
this morning. The path, well-beaten,
traveled as often as some sidewalks,
follows a running creek, into

the millstream, into the Kaw. I sense
an ally in the aged cottonwoods, limbs
wide, trunks thick, grooved with
heavy bark, the footpath bending,

pivoting around them. The voices
of other hikers are socially distanced,
some as much in touch with
cell phones as with blue wood phlox.

Yoga-skinned college students,
all smiles, healthy, vigorous with
future, muscled like the season,
the spring in saplings, in green vines,

have what I cannot find,
a bounding step, a leaf's vigor.
Possibly, it lies ahead around
the next cottonwood. If I could see

clearly beyond my walking stick,
maybe a fox, or a bobcat,

would back away, crouch into
the velvet nothing. However, even
from good eyes, they stay hidden,
as invisible as tomorrow.

May 20, 2020

The Beet Eaters

When I was a small boy, we lived in
married student housing, rows of
Navy barracks left from the war.
They were in constant need of a wrench
or hammer. I followed the workers
like a dog, squatting with them
under houses, laying on my belly
in crawl spaces, sitting on the bottom
rung of a ladder. I was captivated
by their stories, the rough language
they suggested I not repeat. If they
spoke of the war, I do not remember.
Probably, it was left for the night,
tucked in recesses that a pipe wrench
or a saw blade could not reach.
One fellow, I think a plumber's helper,
asked if I wanted to come to East Town
and play with his children. They had
a dog and a tire swing and a garden
that grew beets and tomatoes.

One afternoon, I was sitting on
the back step, digging a trench through
my mother's marigolds. I looked
up when a horn honked, and there
was the plumber's helper. He said,
You ready to go? And I said, I guess so,

brushing the dirt, smacking my hands
like the carpenters and plumbers.
Several children filled the back seat,
obviously, the beet eaters,
eyeing me, grinning. I had a trench
to finish, and the children looked off.
I was thinking how promises are promises
when my mother threw open the screen door.
I was startled by her speed. She spoke
hard words to the plumber's helper, her leg
shoved against my shoulder. She walked
me back to my trench in the flowers,
and handed me my shovel. I am sure
a lecture followed on Section 8s,
but I have forgotten it, unlike the cape
of her dress, billowing like a flag,
as she covered the distance.

May 21, 2020

Parallel Bars, Phase 2

                              Another
gray morning, as still as a hammer
on a workbench. Building rain.
A few desultory sparrows
singing in hidden branches.
It is Friday and the city is open
for business again. Our neighbor,
a waitress at the local pizza shop,
served two tables yesterday, each
with a single customer. The day before
she had two customers as well,
two tables, two menus, two small pizzas,
and a calzone to go. The delivery truck
kept the oven busy. The take-out phone
rang frequently. This is the return
to normal, small steps, parallel bars
on each side, dead weight
struggling with muscle memory.
                              Fresh
flowers are arranged in brass urns,
American flags on graves, whirligigs
for our people, parents, grandparents,
the great uncle with the arrowhead collection.
We expected better than social distancing,
a longer conversation, a surprise ending,
another season to the Netflix
                              series.

The sixth-grade class graduates
from grade school this morning.
Loving parents tape photographs
of their children to the doors
of their SUVs. A map of the parade
has been sent to family members
through email. We arrive early
to stand and wave, to cheer
the graduates, leaning from the windows,
standing like small town mayors
above the moonroofs. Afterwards,
families meet in backyards,
dress hot dogs in mustard and relish,
some lifting facemasks inch by inch
to take a first bite, to spit a smile.

May 22, 2020

Slow Eggs

Jordan cooks slow eggs in the kitchen.
He stirs them for twenty minutes on low heat
until they are fluffed like marshmallows.
This is one way to begin a day,
taking time to let the sun pull itself up
behind the trees, one way to raise
dreams in a little bacon grease,
like Jesus might have
if pork had been on the menu,

if Judas hadn't been in such a hurry
to stick it to the Romans.
Like with slow eggs, you need to
hold your hunger close
until it has hollowed you
into a cave, or a tomb, or a birth.

May 23, 2020

Cottonmouth

The water snake
slides through
the lake shallows
in a state of constant
emergence, a wrinkle
in the reflection
of oaks, a reoccurring
theme of narrow head
cutting the light, body sub-
merged, a swimming S
muscled up to the edge
of morning, a turn
of plot around
the rocks, the
sunken
limb.
It is early.

There is no one
to shout cottonmouth, to
bring a paddle down like an axe.

May 24, 2020

Sh*t from Shinola

As a teenager, mostly unnoticed
between high school and college, I was fired
from two jobs before finding my place
in demolition, earning tuition by gutting

an apartment building, old private housing,
splintered and crowbarred from a dozen rooms
into a dark and dusty cavern. I measured days
by the pile of two-by-fours, the ripped angles

of sheetrock, and the steel mesh, torn

from bathroom tile. I motorcycled
into the strip pits with a joint, and watched
the sun set from the top of a slag pile,
the wind lifting the damp from my hair.

The slanted sun colored the earth, golden
stratifications, soil and sandstone, shoveled up.
The coal pit below, already in shadow,
waited on the rain, the alkaline fill

that could shine the bottom of a boat.
It would be years before the new pit
could sustain the life of fish. At work,
we were joined by carpenters, old names

in pin-striped overalls. We laughed
at their slow gait, the way
they slumped when standing. Our favorite,
a Lloyd or an Elmer or a Hubert,

framed in a kitchen around his ladder.
He had to saw it in two

to angle it free between the studs.
We laughed for the shine of it, wood-gluing
his lunch box to the floor. He cussed a storm
before sitting on a 100 lb. keg of nails

and unwrapping a hard-boiled egg.

May 25, 2020

Possession Is 9/10 of the Law

Whoever said this first must have
been more of a bully, than a sage.
Another someone, a Sufi probably,
claimed that all we really possess
is what we can save from a sinking ship.
Considering the Titanic, that might
include grandpa's pocket watch.
All ownership is a temporary
contract at best. Who can claim
to keep a cat? Even a parrot, a gold
fish, a grandmother with a head
of steam, they stay until they don't,
then they are off, who knows where,
without so much as a toothbrush,
or a pocket for a comb.

May 26, 2020

Junk Phone Call

The man you are looking for
recently died. So, please
leave a message
at the beep. If after
time has lapsed,
and you still have not
heard the beep, be
patient, it takes
a few heartbeats, even
for a beep to reach us
from the afterlife.
The man you are calling
would love to endorse
your candidate, or
donate to your rally,
or take an all expense
paid trip to Nigeria.
So, do not hang up. I
hear his bare feet
plodding down the hall.
He is bringing the beep
with him. Usually,
he keeps it in the vest
pocket of the suit he
is buried in. It is like
a small silver coin.

                    No matter

which phone number
you use tomorrow, you
can talk the tarnish off it.

May 27, 2020

Opening Hollywood's Pool in the Rain

These guys are not afraid of a little water.
They stand outside their white van, two
in hoodies, one in just a t-shirt, one with a sling.
He appears to be in charge, rubbing his lower back,

crawling into the overloaded van. The others
wait for him to hand out tools, a couple of long poles,
nets, buckets of chemicals. All this time
the rain falls steadily, the tall guy lowers his head

so the rain won't drown his cigarette. Finally,
they are in the back yard behind the fence.
On such a quiet morning, their voices are a quartet,
a forte in laughter, with the punch lines

pianissimo, soft-as-shit. I'd like to scale the fence
and join them. I know a joke or two. I was once

a tenor among small ensembles, cleaning
a pool, or painting a house, or drinking on a porch,
always hungry for the new joke, like the tomorrow
which became today, a solo at the window.

May 28, 2020

On Cruelty

I can only
write this
poem by
sinking into
shit, and
this sickens
me to des-
pair, the

gravity
of a knee,
a thigh, 200
pounds of
muscle, bone,
and blood,

compressed
to pavement,
to the man-made
road hard-
ened soul.

If I wrote this,
I would need
my mother

to help me
to my feet again,
and frankly, I
know suffocation
cannot be for-

gotten, for
having once
felt the knee
compressing

the windpipe,
there is no
poem out

living it.

May 29, 2020

Leaving the Labyrinth

He rebuilt his beater, converted it
to run on reclaimed saturated fat,
bartered from fast food joints.
He drove across America, trailing

the scent of French fries and Egg
McMuffins. Once, he sent me the
photograph of a buffalo, as stoic as
Socrates, as Sitting Bull, as Buddha

with a hash pipe. I hung it
on the wall behind my desk, a taste
of ocean, of sunlight. One afternoon,
he walked into my classroom like

a returning Greek, hair wild,
unkempt as a party. He unbuttoned
his shirt to a new tattoo, the wings
of Icarus emblazoned across his shoulders.

We shared some high school coffee,
laughed at what he called the buffalo's
fuck-it eyes. When he left me to my grading,
my stack of senior essays, a wave

of panic hit me. I caught up to him
in the parking lot, under the hood,
tweaking his biscuit and gravy carburetor.
I asked if he knew the whole story.

He cocked his head, smiling
at the warnings of an old Daedalus,
his uninspired flight, the last flicker
of his son falling.

May 30, 2020

Second Childhood Baseball

When I heard my dad say that
old man Simpson had entered
his second childhood, I was eager
to sign up. But second childhoods

only came for the old, and I agreed with
the justice of it. After years of long faces,
pinching for bills, wobbling on canes,
it was only right to get another chance.

Certainly, on base percentages
would improve, the patience to wait
on the right pitch, to take a ball
or drive it into the gap. I discovered

that many of us do not get a second
childhood, some unfortunates go right
on staying old until the end. That was the
pisser that vexed me, tying up the ninth

without extra innings, without a walk-off.
Another popup that I lost in the lights.
No one manages boys like a mother.

Surely, old man Simpson's mother
wasn't chalking the infield. Probably,
she never did. My mother might.
I never missed a breakfast or a lunch.

Dad promised that one day I would find
a girl to marry. If it had happened to him,
he said, it could happen to anyone.
My ticket was to find her, someone to locate

where I had dumped my ball and glove,
someone to sit out the extra innings,
to wash my stirrups and pack my lunch.
Geez, I had a lot to learn about baseball.

May 31, 2020

June

Red Worms

The gardener
trusts the bulb
and the seed,
buried in soil,
watered, and
percolated by
sun. It augers

skyward, grows
into birdsong, blue
feathered, jay
and dove. Invisible,
below the mulch,
the gardener
knows the full
tumble of leaf

and flower, of
vegetable and
herb. She labors,
not unlike the
parent, fingernails
a crescent of topsoil,
of manure, of
yesterday's rot.

She cultivates
the unseen, like
a teacher, an
artist, a carpenter
arranging bones,
banana peels, potato
skins, building
tomorrow out of
compost, out of
worms.

June 1, 2020

Making Plaster Casts in the Strip Pits

I have never seen a wolf in the wild,
coyotes, yes, packs of them, yelping
from the hedgerows, crouched in the strip pits,
loping through the beanfields, dog-eared
on a highway between eighteen wheelers.

But never a wolf, except in nature programs,
television from Mutual of Omaha, Disney.
I've never even real-timed a wolf, lifting his throat
to the moon, howling in ancestral melancholia.

Once as a boy we were making plaster casts
at the state park, coyotes, raccoons, a muskrat.
There was one of a large dog that Ed insisted
had to be a wolf, pad-splayed, deep-clawed.

We kept the cast special, the mud smudged
from the plaster like a dream in the afternoon.

I think we all feared it was just a big dog,
probably with a name like Sarge or King,
but a wolf cast was worth keeping, something
special, like a chunk of pyrite, or a flat rock
that could have been an arrowhead. As boys

we read books on wolves, Indians, earned
merit badges on citizenship, pioneering, but never

a badge for melancholia or howling, never
an embroidered patch for realism. Our leaders
were wise. We kept the casts wrapped in tissue paper,

saved in a shoebox with the make-believe wolves,
the gold that wasn't gold, the fiction of arrowheads.

June 2, 2020

Invoking the Muse in a Public Toilet

The bathroom at the flea market
was marked closed, barricaded with
a yellow plastic sign that read,
No entrada por favor, the same again

in English. I respect signs, having
worked my way through college, scrubbing
the silences, the roadmaps. That said,

I broke the rule and gave the janitor
the slip. He was bent over the sink,
working Comet into the drain,

hard at it, head bobbing
to the rhythm of his elbow. When
he heard me close the stall door,
a string of expletives followed,
rebuffing the chrome faucets,

the shinning knobs, the latch itself.
I tried to explain that it was not
the poet on the toilet,
who was disrespectful of his jazz,
but a plutocratic intestinal track,

more in demand, then any adherence
to signs, even those written in two languages.

All art is given by the Muse. Once invoked,
she is a capricious minx, often
puckish with scat.

June 3, 2020